Waffle Recipes

A Breakfast cookbook with Delicious Waffle Recipes

By
BookSumo Press
All rights reserved

Published by
http://www.booksumo.com

ENJOY THE RECIPES?
KEEP ON COOKING WITH 6 MORE FREE COOKBOOKS!

Visit our website and simply enter your email address to join the club and receive your 6 cookbooks.

http://booksumo.com/magnet

https://www.instagram.com/booksumopress/

https://www.facebook.com/booksumo/

LEGAL NOTES

All Rights Reserved. No Part Of This Book May Be Reproduced Or Transmitted In Any Form Or By Any Means. Photocopying, Posting Online, And / Or Digital Copying Is Strictly Prohibited Unless Written Permission Is Granted By The Book's Publishing Company. Limited Use Of The Book's Text Is Permitted For Use In Reviews Written For The Public.

Table of Contents

Hudson Valley Fruit Waffle Pudding 7

Tex-Mex Cornbread Waffles 8

Strawberry Waffles 9

American Applesauce Waffles 10

Peanut Butter Waffles 11

Margarita's Meringue Waffles 12

Simply Grated Waffles 13

Brazilian Banana Waffles 14

Arizona Waffles 15

10-Minute College Waffles 16

Waffles in Norway 17

Raspberry Fall Waffles 18

Rye Waffles 19

Oatmeal Waffles 20

Belgian Fruit Waffles 21

How to Make a Waffle 22

Flat Waffle Cookies 23

Waffles French Toast Style II 24

November Gingerbread Waffles 25

Cinnamon Ginger Waffles 26

Skytop Waffles 27

PB&J Waffles 28

Maryland Chicken Waffles 29

Cake Flour Waffles 31

Simple Vanilla Waffles 32

Georgia Peach and Biscuit Waffles 33

Dijon Buttermilk Waffles 35

Waffle Sandwiches 36

Country Crispy Waffles 37

Green Feta Waffles 38

Leftover Rice Waffles with Spiced Syrup 39

Lunch Pizza Waffles 40

4-Ingredient American Breakfast 41

Sweet Mediterranean Waffles 42

Cornmeal Cereal Waffles 43

Honey Hazel Waffles 44

Vegetarian Soy Waffles 45

Rachela's Red Velvet Waffles 46

Canadian Chocolate Waffles 47

Cute Waffles 48

Vegan Papaya and Orange Waffles 49

Spicy Cheddar Waffles 50

Seattle Waffles with Avocados 51

Full Georgia Breakfast 52

Waffles Brulee 53

Saratoga Flax Waffles 54

Yuan's Chinese Egg Waffles 55

Hudson Valley
Fruit Waffle Pudding

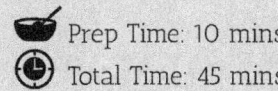 Prep Time: 10 mins
Total Time: 45 mins

Servings per Recipe: 6
Calories   1003.1
Fat   61.0g
Cholesterol   308.2mg
Sodium   861.2mg
Carbohydrates   96.5g
Protein   19.6g

Ingredients

12 waffles, cubed
300 g raspberries,
200 g white chocolate, chopped
1/4 C. caster sugar
1 tbsp plain flour
3 eggs
1 tsp grated lemon rind
1 tsp vanilla extract
500 ml thickened cream
2 tbsp icing sugar

Directions

1. Set your oven to 350 degrees F before doing anything else and grease a baking dish.
2. In a bowl, add the flour, sugar, lemon rind, cream, eggs and vanilla and beat until well combined.
3. In the bottom of the prepared baking dish, arrange half of the waffles.
4. Place half of raspberries over the waffles evenly, followed by half of the chocolate.
5. Repeat the layers once and top with the egg mixture evenly.
6. Keep aside for about 10-12 minutes.
7. Cook in the oven for about 35 minutes.
8. Enjoy with a dusting of the icing sugar.

TEX-MEX Cornbread Waffles

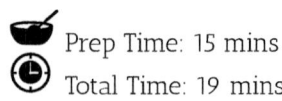

Prep Time: 15 mins
Total Time: 19 mins

Servings per Recipe: 9
Calories   237.7
Fat   10.8g
Cholesterol   52.6mg
Sodium   358.6mg
Carbohydrates   28.1g
Protein   7.7g

Ingredients

1 C. cornmeal
1 C. all-purpose flour
2 1/2 tsp baking powder
1 tsp xanthan gum
1 tbsp sugar
1 tsp cumin
1/4 tsp baking soda
1/2 tsp salt
5 tbsp dry buttermilk
1 1/4-1 1/2 C. water

1/4 C. vegetable oil
2 large eggs, separated
1 medium ear corn on the cob, kernels cut off
2/3 C. grated sharp cheddar cheese
1 - 2 medium jalapeño peppers, diced

Directions

1. Set your waffle iron and lightly, grease it.
2. In a bowl, add the cornmeal, flour, xanthan gum, sugar, buttermilk powder, baking powder, baking soda, cumin and salt and mix until well combined.
3. In another bowl, add the egg yolks, oil and 1 1/4 C. of the warm water and beat until well combined.
4. Add the flour mixture and mix until well combined.
5. Add the cheese, corn and peppers and gently, stir to combine.
6. In a glass bowl, add the egg whites and beat until stiff peaks form.
7. Gently, fold the whipped egg whites into the flour mixture.
8. Add desired amount of the mixture in waffle iron and cook as suggested by the manufacturer.
9. Repeat with the remaining mixture.
10. Enjoy warm.

Strawberry Waffles

Prep Time: 15 mins
Total Time: 20 mins

Servings per Recipe: 3
Calories   228.1
Fat   4.4g
Cholesterol   70.9mg
Sodium   256.7mg
Carbohydrates   39.2g
Protein   9.0g

Ingredients

1/2 C. whole wheat flour
1/2 C. all-purpose flour
2 tbsp ground flax seeds
2 tsp sugar substitute
1 tsp baking powder
1/8 tsp salt
1 C. sliced strawberry
1/4 C. skim milk
2 tbsp natural applesauce
1/2 tsp vanilla extract
1 large egg

Directions

1. Set your waffle iron and lightly, grease it.
2. In a bowl, add the flax seed, flours, Splenda, baking powder and salt and mix well.
3. With a spoon, create a well in the middle of the flour mixture.
4. In a food processor, add the strawberries, egg, applesauce, milk and vanilla and pulse until pureed.
5. Add the pureed mixture into the well of the flour mixture and mix until just combined.
6. Add 1/2 C. of the mixture in waffle iron and cook for about 5 minutes.
7. Repeat with the remaining mixture.
8. Enjoy warm.

AMERICAN
Applesauce Waffles

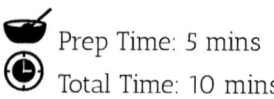
Prep Time: 5 mins
Total Time: 10 mins

Servings per Recipe: 8
Calories 345.5
Fat 4.3g
Cholesterol 110.3mg
Sodium 223.8mg
Carbohydrates 64.6g
Protein 13.6g

Ingredients

3/4 C. applesauce
2 C. unbleached all-purpose flour
2 C. whole wheat flour
3 tsp baking powder
4 tbsp brown sugar
1 tsp ground cinnamon
1/4 tsp ground cloves

1/4 tsp ground nutmeg
4 eggs
3 C. low-fat milk
1/2 C. apple juice
2 tbsp ginger, grated

Directions

1. Set your waffle iron and lightly, grease it.
2. In a bowl, add the flours, sugar, baking powder and spices and mix well.
3. In a separate bowl, add the remaining ingredients and beat until well combined.
4. Add the flour mixture and mix until just combined.
5. Add desired amount of the mixture in waffle iron and cook as suggested by the manufacturer.
6. Repeat with the remaining mixture.
7. Enjoy warm.

Peanut Butter Waffles

Prep Time: 15 mins
Total Time: 20 mins

Servings per Recipe: 6	
Calories	453.1
Fat	25.6g
Cholesterol	71.1mg
Sodium	477.3mg
Carbohydrates	44.9g
Protein	16.3g

Ingredients

2 1/4 C. whole wheat flour
4 tsp baking powder
1/2 C. creamy peanut butter
1 1/2 tbsp sugar
2 eggs, beaten
2 1/4 C. whole milk
1/4 C. vegetable oil
1/4 tsp kosher salt
cooking spray

Directions

1. Set your waffle iron and lightly, grease it with the cooking spray.
2. In the bowl of an electric mixer, fitted with the paddle attachment, add the remaining ingredients and mix until well combined.
3. Add desired amount of the mixture in waffle iron and cook for about 4-5 minutes.
4. Repeat with the remaining mixture.
5. Enjoy warm.

MARGARITA'S
Meringue Waffles

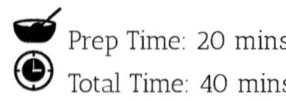

Prep Time: 20 mins
Total Time: 40 mins

Servings per Recipe: 6
Calories   248.8
Fat   7.8g
Cholesterol   56.3mg
Sodium   350.1mg
Carbohydrates   35.7g
Protein   8.0g

Ingredients

Waffle
2 C. plain flour
1/2 tsp baking soda
1/2 tsp salt
2 tbsp extra granulated sugar
1 egg, separated
1 1/4 C. milk
1/8 C. unsalted butter, melted
2 tsp grated lemon zest
Garnish
12 tbsp yogurt
12 tbsp lemon curd
12 small meringues, crushed
mint leaf

Directions

1. Set your waffle iron and lightly, grease it.
2. In a bowl, add the flour, sugar, baking soda, salt and mix well.
3. With a spoon, create a well in the middle of the flour mixture.
4. Add the milk and egg yolk in the well of the flour mixture and with a whisk, mix until well combined
5. Add the butter and lemon zest and gently, stir to combine.
6. In a glass bowl, add the egg whites and beat until stiff peaks form.
7. Gently, fold the whipped egg whites into the flour mixture.
8. Add desired amount of the mixture in waffle iron and cook as suggested by the manufacturer.
9. Repeat with the remaining mixture.
10. Meanwhile, for the topping: in a bowl, add the lemon curd and yogurt and stir to combine.
11. Divide the waffles onto serving plates.
12. Place a dollop of the yogurt mixture over each waffle.
13. Enjoy with a topping of the meringue and mint leaves.

Simply Grated Waffles

Prep Time: 15 mins
Total Time: 35 mins

Servings per Recipe: 4
Calories   413.0
Fat   15.1g
Cholesterol   140.7mg
Sodium   904.7mg
Carbohydrates   53.7g
Protein   14.9g

Ingredients

2 C. flour
4 tsp baking powder
1/2 tsp salt
2 eggs
1 1/4 C. milk
2 tbsp melted butter
1/2 C. of grated cheese

Directions

1. Set your waffle iron and lightly, grease it.
2. In a bowl, sift together the flour, baking powder and salt.
3. In another bowl, add the milk and egg yolks and beat well.
4. In the bowl of the flour mixture, add the milk mixture, and mix well.
5. Add the butter and mix well.
6. Add the cheese and gently, stir to combine.
7. In a glass bowl, add the egg whites and beat until stiff peaks form.
8. Gently, fold the whipped egg whites into the flour mixture.
9. Add desired amount of the mixture in waffle iron and cook as suggested by the manufacturer.
10. Repeat with the remaining mixture.
11. Enjoy warm.

BRAZILIAN
Banana Waffles

Prep Time: 5 mins
Total Time: 20 mins

Servings per Recipe: 4
Calories 558.1
Fat 33.3g
Cholesterol 95.8mg
Sodium 494.9mg
Carbohydrates 53.5g
Protein 11.9g

Ingredients

1 3/4 C. all-purpose flour
1 tbsp baking powder
1 tsp ground cinnamon
1/4 tsp nutmeg
1/4 tsp salt
2 egg yolks
1 1/2 C. milk
2/3 C. banana, ripened and mashed

1/2 C. cooking oil
2 egg whites

Directions

1. In a bowl, add the flour, spices, baking powder and salt and mix well.
2. In another bowl, add the oil, milk, egg yolks and banana and beat until well combined.
3. Slowly, add the flour mixture and mix until just combined.
4. In a glass bowl, add the egg whites and beat until stiff peaks form.
5. Gently, fold the whipped egg whites into the flour mixture.
6. Add 1-1 1/4 C. of the mixture in waffle iron and cook as suggested by the manufacturer.
7. Repeat with the remaining mixture.
8. Enjoy warm.

Arizona Waffles

Prep Time: 8 mins
Total Time: 16 mins

Servings per Recipe: 4
Calories   746.5
Fat   43.4g
Cholesterol   153.4mg
Sodium   1338.1mg
Carbohydrates   68.7g
Protein   26.9g

Ingredients

1 1/2 C. all-purpose flour
1/2 C. yellow cornmeal
1 1/3 C. longhorn cheese, grated
1 tbsp baking powder
2 tsp sugar
1/2 tsp salt
1 tsp mild chili powder

1 2/3 C. milk
2 eggs, beaten
1/3 C. vegetable oil
2 tbsp chopped green chilies

Directions

1. Set your waffle iron and lightly, grease it.
2. In a bowl, add the cheese, cornmeal, flour, sugar, baking powder, chili powder and salt and mix well
3. Add the eggs, oil, milk and chilies and beat until just combined.
4. Add desired amount of the mixture in waffle iron and cook as suggested by the manufacturer.
5. Repeat with the remaining mixture.
6. Enjoy warm.

10-MINUTE
College Waffles

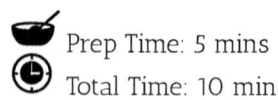

Prep Time: 5 mins
Total Time: 10 mins

Servings per Recipe: 4
Calories 516.0
Fat 37.7g
Cholesterol 54.0mg
Sodium 799.6mg
Carbohydrates 38.0g
Protein 6.3g

Ingredients

2 C. Bisquick
1 1/3 C. club soda
1 egg
1/2 C. oil

Directions

1. Set your waffle iron and lightly, grease it.
2. In a bowl, add all the ingredients and mix until well combined.
3. Add desired amount of the mixture in waffle iron and cook as suggested by the manufacturer.
4. Repeat with the remaining mixture.
5. Enjoy warm.

Waffles in Norway

Prep Time: 15 mins
Total Time: 25 mins

Servings per Recipe: 8
Calories   276.3
Fat   13.8g
Cholesterol   100.8mg
Sodium   251.7mg
Carbohydrates   32.3g
Protein   6.0g

Ingredients

- 3 eggs, lightly beaten
- 1/2 C. sugar
- 1 (16 oz.) containers sour cream
- 1 1/2 C. flour
- 1 pinch salt
- 1 tsp baking soda
- 1/2 tsp ground cardamom
- strawberry jam

Directions

1. In a bowl, add the sugar and eggs and beat until fluffy.
2. Add the remaining ingredients and mix until just combined.
3. Keep aside for about 9-10 minutes.
4. Set your waffle iron and lightly, grease it.
5. Add desired amount of the mixture in waffle iron and cook as suggested by the manufacturer.
6. Repeat with the remaining mixture.
7. Enjoy warm with a topping of the strawberry jam.

RASPBERRY
Fall Waffles

Prep Time: 8 mins
Total Time: 18 mins

Servings per Recipe: 12
Calories	171.2
Fat	6.5g
Cholesterol	39.5mg
Sodium	203.7mg
Carbohydrates	24.2g
Protein	3.9g

Ingredients

1 1/2 C. all-purpose flour
1 tbsp sugar
2 1/2 tsp baking powder
1/2 tsp salt
2 eggs
1 1/2 C. milk

2 tbsp vegetable oil
1/2 C. raspberry preserves
1/3 C. chopped pecans

Directions

1. In a microwave-safe bowl, add the raspberry preserves and microwave for about 1 minute.
2. In a bowl, add the flour, baking powder, sugar and salt and mix well.
3. In another bowl, add the oil, milk and eggs and beat until well combined.
4. Add the flour mixture and mix until just combined.
5. Gently, fold in the warm raspberry preserves and pecans and mix until just blended.
6. Add desired amount of the mixture in waffle iron and cook as suggested by the manufacturer.
7. Repeat with the remaining mixture.
8. Enjoy warm.

Rye Waffles

Prep Time: 30 mins
Total Time: 30 mins

Servings per Recipe: 1
Calories	2558.3
Fat	129.7g
Cholesterol	684.3mg
Sodium	5297.5mg
Carbohydrates	304.1g
Protein	60.5g

Ingredients

2 C. milk
1 tbsp lemon juice
2 eggs
2 tsp sugar
2 C. cornmeal
1 C. rye flour

1/2 C. butter, melted
2 tbsp baking powder
1 tsp baking soda
1/4 tsp salt

Directions

1. In a bowl, add the cornmeal, rye, sugar, eggs and butter and mix until well combined.
2. Keep aside for about 14-15 minutes.
3. Set your waffle iron and lightly, grease it.
4. Add the lemon juice and mix well.
5. Add the baking powder and baking soda and mix well.
6. Add desired amount of the mixture in waffle iron and cook as suggested by the manufacturer.
7. Repeat with the remaining mixture.
8. Enjoy warm.

OATMEAL
Waffles

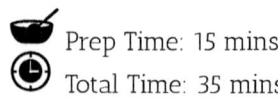

Prep Time: 15 mins
Total Time: 35 mins

Servings per Recipe: 6
Calories   397.6
Fat   19.0g
Cholesterol   113.6mg
Sodium   602.4mg
Carbohydrates   48.1g
Protein   10.5g

Ingredients

1 C. oatmeal
2 tbsp toasted wheat germ
1/2 C. butter, melted
2 eggs, beaten
1/4 C. honey
1 C. all-purpose flour
1/2 C. whole wheat flour

1 tsp baking soda
1/2 tsp salt
1 1/2 C. buttermilk
butter
syrup

Directions

1. Set your waffle iron and lightly, grease it.
2. In a bowl, add the wheat germ and cereal and mix well.
3. In a second bowl, add the flours, salt and baking soda and mix well.
4. In a third bowl, add the honey, eggs and butter and beat until well combined.
5. Add the cereal mixture and mix well.
6. Add the flour mixture, alternating with the buttermilk and mix until a very stiff mixture is formed.
7. Add desired amount of the mixture in waffle iron and cook as suggested by the manufacturer.
8. Repeat with the remaining mixture.
9. Enjoy warm with a topping of the butter and syrup.

Belgian Fruit Waffles

Prep Time: 10 mins
Total Time: 20 mins

Servings per Recipe: 6
Calories   375.5
Fat   13.8g
Cholesterol   103.2mg
Sodium   431.5mg
Carbohydrates   54.9g
Protein   8.2g

Ingredients

1/3 C. butter
1/2 C. sugar
2 large eggs
2 C. flour
2 tsp baking powder
1/2 tsp salt

1 C. milk
1 1/2 C. sliced peaches, chopped
1/2 tsp vanilla
1/2 tsp lemon juice

Directions

1. Set your waffle iron and lightly, grease it.
2. In a glass bowl, add the sugar and butter and beat until creamy.
3. Add the eggs and whisk until blended nicely.
4. In another bowl, sift together the flour, salt and baking powder.
5. Add the egg mixture, milk, vanilla and lemon juice and mix until well combined.
6. Gently, fold in the peach pieces.
7. Add desired amount of the mixture in waffle iron and cook as suggested by the manufacturer.
8. Repeat with the remaining mixture.
9. Enjoy warm.

HOW TO
a Waffle

Prep Time: 5 mins
Total Time: 10 mins

Servings per Recipe: 4
Calories	581.8
Fat	33.0g
Cholesterol	67.8mg
Sodium	724.8mg
Carbohydrates	60.1g
Protein	11.5g

Ingredients

2 C. flour
4 tsp baking powder
1/2 tsp salt
2 tbsp sugar
1/2 C. vegetable oil

1 3/4 C. milk
1 egg

Directions

1. In a bowl, sift together the flour and baking powder.
2. Add the sugar and salt and mix well.
3. Add the remaining ingredients and mix until well combined.
4. Add desired amount of the mixture in waffle iron and cook for about 5-6 minutes.
5. Repeat with the remaining mixture.
6. Enjoy warm.

Flat Waffle Cookies (Pizelles)

Prep Time: 10 mins
Total Time: 40 mins

Servings per Recipe: 60
Calories   95.2
Fat   3.9g
Cholesterol   21.1mg
Sodium   49.1mg
Carbohydrates   13.2g
Protein   1.5g

Ingredients

6 large eggs, beaten
2 C. granulated sugar
1/2 C. margarine, melted and cooled
1/2 C. canola oil
1 tsp vanilla
1 tsp almond extract
3 tbsp anise extract
4 C. all-purpose white flour
4 tsp baking powder
powdered sugar

Directions

1. Set your pizelle iron and lightly, grease it.
2. In a bowl, mix together the flour and baking powder.
3. In another bowl, add the sugar and eggs and beat until creamy.
4. Add the margarine and mix well.
5. Slowly, add the flour mixture, 1 C. at a time and mix until just combined.
6. Add desired amount of the mixture in waffle iron and cook as suggested by the manufacturer.
7. Repeat with the remaining mixture.
8. Enjoy warm with a dusting of the powdered sugar.

WAFFLES
French Toast Style II

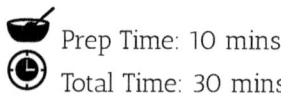

Prep Time: 10 mins
Total Time: 30 mins

Servings per Recipe: 4
Calories   804.8
Fat   13.2g
Cholesterol   114.6mg
Sodium   1650.9mg
Carbohydrates   139.9g
Protein   28.1g

Ingredients

1 C. skim milk
1 tbsp sugar
1 tbsp butter, melted
1 tsp vanilla
1/2 tsp cinnamon

2 eggs
16 slices day-old French bread
cooking spray

Directions

1. Set your waffle iron and lightly, grease it.
2. In a bowl, add the butter, sugar, eggs, milk, vanilla and cinnamon and beat until well combined.
3. In the bottom of a 13x9-inch baking dish, arrange the bread slices evenly.
4. Top with the milk mixture and gently, coat the bread pieces with mixture.
5. Keep side for about 5 minutes.
6. Arrange 4 bread slices in the waffle iron. and cook for about 4-5 minutes.
7. Repeat with the remaining bread slices.

November
Gingerbread Waffles

Prep Time: 15 mins
Total Time: 30 mins

Servings per Recipe: 8
Calories   209.2
Fat   7.2g
Cholesterol   26.4mg
Sodium   208.0mg
Carbohydrates   34.2g
Protein   2.4g

Ingredients

1/4 C. sugar
1/4 C. shortening
1 egg
1/2 C. molasses
1 C. all-purpose flour
3/4 tsp baking soda
1/4 tsp salt
1 tsp ground ginger
1/2 tsp ground cinnamon
1/4 tsp ground cloves
1/2 C. hot water
sweetened whipped cream
ground cinnamon

Directions

1. Set your waffle iron and lightly, grease it.
2. In a bowl, add the flour, baking soda, spices and salt and mix well.
3. In another bowl, add the shortening and sugar and beat until creamy.
4. Add the molasses and beat until blended nicely.
5. Add the flour mixture and beat until well combined.
6. Add the hot water and stir to combine.
7. Add 1 1/4 C. of the mixture in waffle iron and cook as suggested by the manufacturer.
8. Repeat with the remaining mixture.
9. Enjoy warm a topping of the whipped cream and extra cinnamon.

CINNAMON
Ginger Waffles

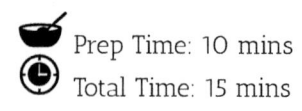

🥣 Prep Time: 10 mins
🕐 Total Time: 15 mins

Servings per Recipe: 8
Calories 492.6
Fat 15.8g
Cholesterol 128.8mg
Sodium 641.9mg
Carbohydrates 79.3g
Protein 9.7g

Ingredients

3 C. all-purpose flour
4 tsp baking powder
2 tsp ground cinnamon
1 1/2 tsp ginger, grated
1 tsp salt
4 eggs
2/3 C. brown sugar, packed

2 medium bananas, extra-ripe
1 1/4 C. milk
1/2 C. molasses
1/2 C. butter, melted
powdered sugar

Directions

1. Set your waffle iron and lightly, grease it.
2. In a food processor, add the bananas and pulse until pureed.
3. In a bowl, add the flour, spices, baking powder and salt.
4. In another bowl, add the brown sugar and eggs and beat until creamy.
5. Add the corn syrup, molasses, milk and pureed bananas and beat until well combined.
6. Add the flour mixture and mix until just combined.
7. Add 3/4 C. of the mixture in waffle iron and cook as suggested by the manufacturer.
8. Repeat with the remaining mixture.
9. Enjoy warm with a sprinkling of the powdered sugar.

Skytop Waffles

Prep Time: 5 mins
Total Time: 8 mins

Servings per Recipe: 1
Calories	3840.5
Fat	226.5g
Cholesterol	1633.4mg
Sodium	8508.2mg
Carbohydrates	362.4g
Protein	106.0g

Ingredients

- 1 1/2 C. buckwheat flour
- 1 1/2 C. flour
- 4 tsp baking powder
- 1 1/2 tsp baking soda
- 1 tsp salt
- 4 tbsp sugar
- 6 eggs
- 3 C. buttermilk
- 1 C. melted and cooled butter

Directions

1. Set your waffle iron and lightly, grease it.
2. In a bowl, add the flours, baking soda, baking powder, sugar and salt and mix well.
3. In another bowl, add the butter, eggs and buttermilk and beat until blended nicely.
4. Add the flour mixture and mix until just combined.
5. Add desired amount of the mixture in waffle iron and cook as suggested by the manufacturer.
6. Repeat with the remaining mixture.
7. Enjoy warm.

PB&J Waffles

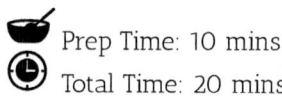

Prep Time: 10 mins
Total Time: 20 mins

Servings per Recipe: 10
Calories	187.2
Fat	10.0g
Cholesterol	50.6mg
Sodium	239.7mg
Carbohydrates	19.2g
Protein	6.0g

Ingredients

1 1/4 C. all-purpose flour
3 tbsp sugar
1 tbsp baking powder
1/4 tsp baking soda
1/4 tsp ground cinnamon
2 eggs, separated
1 1/4 C. milk

1/3 C. peanut butter
3 tbsp butter, melted
jelly

Directions

1. In a bowl, add the flour, sugar, baking soda, baking powder and cinnamon and mix well.
2. In another bowl, add the butter, peanut butter, milk and egg yolks and beat until well combined.
3. Add the flour mixture and mix until just combined.
4. In a glass bowl, add the egg whites and beat until stiff peaks form.
5. Gently, fold the whipped egg whites into the flour mixture.
6. Add the flour mixture and mix until just combined.
7. Add desired amount of the mixture in waffle iron and cook as suggested by the manufacturer.
8. Repeat with the remaining mixture.
9. Enjoy warm with a topping of the jelly.

Maryland Chicken Waffles

🥣 Prep Time: 12 hrs
🕐 Total Time: 12 hrs 20 mins

Servings per Recipe: 2
Calories   904.6
Fat   59.4g
Cholesterol   95.8mg
Sodium   1057.3mg
Carbohydrates   53.4g
Protein   37.6g

Ingredients

8 oz. chicken breasts, chucks
1/4 C. buttermilk
1/2 tsp seasoning salt
1/4 tsp ground black pepper
1/4 tsp paprika
1/4 C. canola oil
1 C. panko breadcrumbs

8 slices turkey bacon
2 Pillsbury grands refrigerated biscuits
maple syrup

Directions

1. In a bowl, add the buttermilk, chicken pieces, seasoned salt, paprika and black pepper and mix well.
2. Refrigerate to marinate for whole night.
3. Remove the chicken pieces from the marinade and coat with the breadcrumbs evenly.
4. Place a large skillet over high heat until heated through.
5. Add the bacon and cook for about 8-10 minutes.
6. With a slotted spoon, place the bacon onto a paper towel-lined plate to drain.
7. In the same skillet, add the oil with the bacon grease over high heat and cook the chicken pieces for about 3-4 minutes per side.
8. With a slotted spoon, place the chicken into a bowl.
9. Now, crumble the bacon into small pieces and divide into 3 equal sized parts.
10. Open the Pillsbury Biscuits dough packages.
11. Place 1 part of the bacon bits over one dough and with your palms, pat into a 7-inch circle.
12. Repeat with the second dough.
13. Set your waffle iron and lightly, grease it.

14. Arrange 1 dough circle into the waffle iron and cook for about 5 minutes.
15. Repeat with the second dough circle.
16. Arrange the waffles onto serving plates and drizzle with the maple syrup.
17. Divide chicken and remaining bacon part over each waffle and enjoy.

Cake Flour Waffles

Prep Time: 10 mins
Total Time: 15 mins

Servings per Recipe: 1
Calories   271.5
Fat   17.2g
Cholesterol   97.6mg
Sodium   467.0mg
Carbohydrates   23.9g
Protein   5.5g

Ingredients

- 1/2 C. butter, melted
- 1 tbsp sugar
- 2 egg yolks
- 2 egg whites, beaten
- 1 C. buttermilk
- 1 pinch salt
- 1 C. cake flour
- 1 tbsp cake flour
- 4 tsp baking powder

Directions

1. Set your waffle iron and lightly, grease it.
2. In a bowl, sift together the flour, baking powder and salt.
3. In a bowl, add the sugar and butter and beat until creamy.
4. Add the egg yolks and mix well.
5. Add the flour mixture and milk and mix until just combined.
6. In a glass bowl, add the egg whites and beat until stiff peaks form.
7. Gently, fold the whipped egg whites into the flour mixture.
8. Add desired amount of the mixture in waffle iron and cook as suggested by the manufacturer.
9. Repeat with the remaining mixture.
10. Enjoy warm.

SIMPLE
Vanilla Waffles

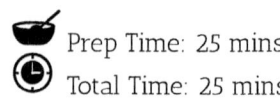

Prep Time: 25 mins
Total Time: 25 mins

Servings per Recipe: 6
Calories	517.2
Fat	27.2g
Cholesterol	189.6mg
Sodium	981.3mg
Carbohydrates	54.0g
Protein	13.5g

Ingredients

3 C. sifted flour
4 tsp double-acting baking powder
1 tsp salt
2 tsp sugar
2/3 C. butter, melted

2 C. milk
4 eggs, separated
1 tsp vanilla

Directions

1. In a bowl, add the flour, sugar, baking powder and salt and mix well.
2. In another bowl, add the milk, egg yolks and vanilla and beat until well combined.
3. Add the flour mixture and mix until just combined.
4. Add the butter and mix until well combined.
5. In a glass bowl, add the egg whites and beat until stiff peaks form.
6. Gently, fold the whipped egg whites into the flour mixture.
7. Add 14 oz. of the mixture in waffle iron and cook as suggested by the manufacturer.
8. Repeat with the remaining mixture.
9. Enjoy warm.

Georgia Peach and Biscuit Waffles

Prep Time: 15 mins
Total Time: 40 mins

Servings per Recipe: 4
Calories   845.3
Fat   41.4g
Cholesterol   63.1mg
Sodium   1641.4mg
Carbohydrates   107.1g
Protein   13.9g

Ingredients

3 oz. cream cheese
1/4 C. ricotta cheese
2 tbsp powdered sugar
1 tsp vanilla extract
1/4 tsp lemon juice
1/4 tsp lemon zest
2 large ripe peaches, halved and pitted
2 (10 count) cans refrigerated biscuits
4 tbsp melted butter
1 tbsp honey
1/2 C. granulated sugar
2 tsp cinnamon
2 pieces Reynolds Wrap Foil

Directions

1. Set your oven to 375 degrees F before doing anything else and arrange 2 foil pieces onto a baking sheet.
2. In a bowl, add the ricotta cheese, cream cheese and powdered sugar and beat until smooth.
3. Add the lemon zest, lemon juice and vanilla and stir until blended nicely.
4. Place in the fridge until using.
5. In a bowl, add 1 tbsp of the honey and 1 tbsp of the butter and mix well.
6. Arrange 2 peach halves onto 1 foil pieces, skin side down.
7. Coat each peach half with the honey mixture evenly.
8. Fold each foil over the peach halves to create a pouch.
9. Cook in the oven for about 15-20 minutes.
10. Set your waffle iron and lightly, grease it.
11. In a shallow plate, place the remaining 3 tbsp of the butter.
12. In another shallow plate, add the granulated sugar and cinnamon and mix well.
13. With the palms of your hands, pat each biscuit and shape into a small disk.

14. Coat each disk with the melted butter and then with the cinnamon sugar.
15. Arrange the coated disks into waffle iron in batches and cook for about 3 minutes.
16. Transfer the cooked waffles onto a platter and with a piece of foil, cover them to keep warm.
17. Remove the peaches from the oven.
18. Careful, open the foil pouches to cool the peaches.
19. Arrange 5 waffles onto each serving plate.
20. Place about 1 tbsp of the cream cheese mixture in the center of each peach half.
21. Carefully, place 1 peach half over the waffles in each plate.
22. Enjoy warm with a drizzling of the remaining honey butter.

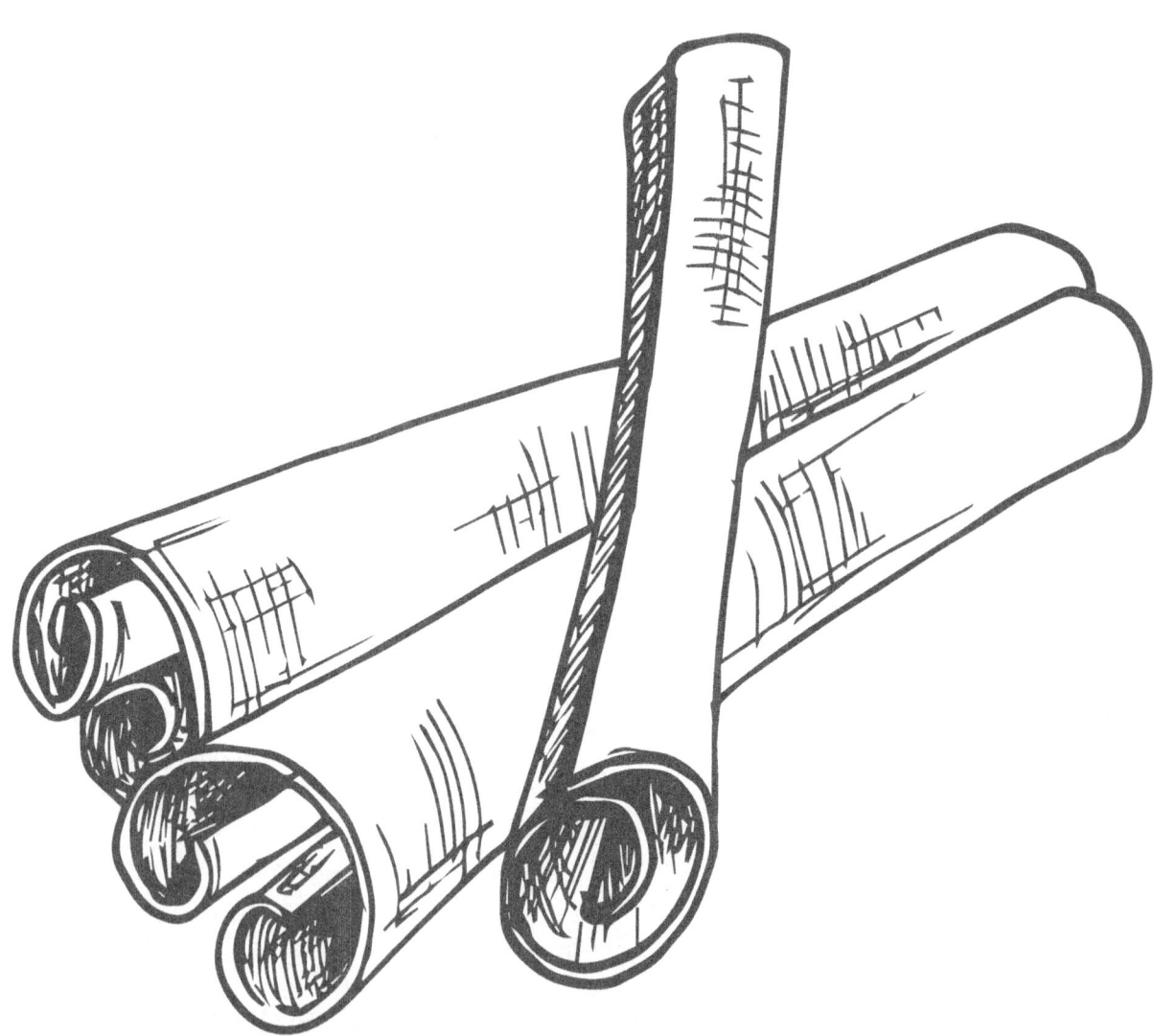

Dijon Buttermilk Waffles

Prep Time: 30 mins
Total Time: 30 mins

Servings per Recipe: 4
Calories	335.5
Fat	16.3g
Cholesterol	145.7mg
Sodium	740.3mg
Carbohydrates	33.0g
Protein	14.3g

Ingredients

- 2/3 C. flour
- 2/3 C. rye flour
- 1/4 tsp baking soda
- 1 tsp baking powder
- 1/2 tsp salt
- 2 eggs, beaten
- 1 C. buttermilk
- 2 tbsp melted butter
- 2 tbsp chopped scallions
- 1/2 tsp Dijon mustard
- 3/4 C. grated smoked cheddar cheese

Directions

1. In a bowl, add the flours, baking powder, baking soda and salt.
2. In another bowl, add the cheese, butter, buttermilk, eggs, mustard and scallions and beat until well combined.
3. Add the flour mixture and mix until just blended.
4. Keep the mixture aside for about 9-10 minutes.
5. Set your waffle iron and lightly, grease it.
6. Add 1/3 C. of the mixture in waffle iron and cook as suggested by the manufacturer.
7. Repeat with the remaining mixture.
8. Enjoy warm.

WAFFLE
Sandwiches

Prep Time: 15 mins
Total Time: 30 mins

Servings per Recipe: 4
Calories 780.5
Fat 32.2g
Cholesterol 57.4mg
Sodium 629.0mg
Carbohydrates 117.7g
Protein 9.4g

Ingredients

8 frozen waffles
2 (3 oz.) packages cream cheese, softened
1/2 C. packed brown sugar
1/2 tsp ground cinnamon
1 tsp vanilla extract
1/2 C. chopped pecans
1 C. maple syrup
confectioners' sugar
4 strawberries, halved

Directions

1. In a bowl, add the cream cheese, vanilla, brown sugar and cinnamon and beat until smooth.
2. Add the pecans and stir to combine.
3. Toast the waffles as suggested on the package.
4. Arrange 4 waffles onto serving plates.
5. Place cream cheese mixture over these waffles evenly and cover with the remaining waffles.
6. Drizzle each waffle sandwich with the maple syrup and dust with the confectioners' sugar.
7. Enjoy with a garnishing of the fruit.

Country Crispy Waffles

Prep Time: 11 mins
Total Time: 15 mins

Servings per Recipe: 1
Calories   310.4
Fat   16.6g
Cholesterol   52.9mg
Sodium   383.8mg
Carbohydrates   34.5g
Protein   5.1g

Ingredients

- 1 1/4 C. all-purpose flour
- 1 C. rice krispies cereal
- 3/4 C. cornstarch
- 1/4 C. sugar
- 1 tsp baking powder
- 1/2 tsp baking soda
- 3/4 tsp table salt
- 2 large eggs, separated
- 1 1/2 C. milk
- 1 tsp vanilla extract
- 1/2 C. vegetable oil

Directions

1. Set your waffle iron to medium setting and lightly, grease it.
2. In a bowl, add the cornstarch, Rice Krispies, flour, sugar, baking soda, baking powder and salt and mix well.
3. In another bowl, add the oil, milk, egg yolks and vanilla and beat until well combined.
4. add the flour mixture and mix until just combined.
5. In a glass bowl, add the egg whites and beat until soft peaks form.
6. Gently, fold the whipped egg whites into the flour mixture.
7. Add 2/3 C. of the mixture in waffle iron and cook for about 3-4 minutes.
8. Repeat with the remaining mixture.
9. Enjoy warm.

GREEN FETA
Waffles

Prep Time: 15 mins
Total Time: 15 mins

Servings per Recipe: 1
Calories	633.4
Fat	38.6g
Cholesterol	128.0mg
Sodium	691.8mg
Carbohydrates	55.0g
Protein	16.3g

Ingredients

1 egg, separated
1 C. all-purpose flour
1 tsp baking powder
1/8 tsp salt
1/2-1 tsp sugar
1/8 tsp garlic powder
1/4 tsp dried dill
3/4 C. milk
1/3 C. crumbled feta cheese
1/3 C. cooked spinach, well drained and chopped
4 tbsp olive oil

Directions

1. Set your waffle iron and lightly, grease it.
2. In a bowl, add the flour, sugar, baking powder, dried dill, garlic powder and salt and mix well.
3. In another bowl, add the oil, milk, egg yolk and feta cheese and mix until well combined.
4. Add the flour mixture and mix until just combined.
5. In a glass bowl, add the egg whites and beat until stiff peaks form.
6. Gently, fold the whipped egg whites into the flour mixture.
7. Add the flour mixture and mix until just combined.
8. Add desired amount of the mixture in waffle iron and cook as suggested by the manufacturer.
9. Repeat with the remaining mixture.
10. Enjoy warm.

Leftover Rice Waffles with Spiced Syrup

Prep Time: 15 mins
Total Time: 23 mins

Servings per Recipe: 1
Calories   304.5
Fat   8.1g
Cholesterol   66.7mg
Sodium   383.2mg
Carbohydrates   54.8g
Protein   4.8g

Ingredients

1 C. sifted flour
2 tsp baking powder
2 tbsp sugar
3/4 tsp salt
2 egg yolks, beaten
1 C. milk
2 tbsp melted butter
1 C. cooked rice
2 egg whites, beaten

Flavored Syrup
1/2 C. honey
1/2 C. maple syrup
1/2 tsp caraway seed
1 tsp ground cinnamon
2 tbsp butter

Directions

1. Set your waffle iron and lightly, grease it.
2. In a bowl, add the flour, sugar, baking powder and salt and mix well. Now, sift the flour mixture into another bowl.
3. In another bowl, add the butter, milk and egg yolks and beat until well combined.
4. Add the flour mixture and mix until just combined.
5. In a glass bowl, add the egg whites and beat until stiff peaks form.
6. Gently, fold the cooked rice and whipped egg whites into the flour mixture. Add desired amount of the mixture in waffle iron and cook as suggested by the manufacturer.
7. Repeat with the remaining mixture.
8. Meanwhile, for syrup: in a pan, add the butter, maple syrup, honey, caraway seeds and cinnamon and cook until boiling, stirring continuously. Enjoy the waffles warm with a topping of the syrup.

LUNCH
Pizza Waffles

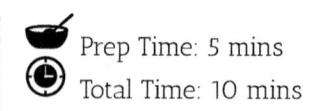

Prep Time: 5 mins
Total Time: 10 mins

Servings per Recipe: 1
Calories 65.1
Fat 3.8g
Cholesterol 11.0mg
Sodium 238.0mg
Carbohydrates 3.8g
Protein 3.7g

Ingredients

1 frozen gluten-free waffle, toasted
2 - 3 tbsp pizza sauce
6 pepperoni slices

2 tbsp mozzarella cheese

Directions

1. Set your oven to broiler.
2. Place the pizza sauce over waffle evenly and top with the pepperoni, followed by the mozzarella cheese.
3. Cook under the broiler until the cheese is melted.
4. Enjoy warm.

4-Ingredient American Breakfast (Quick Waffle Sandwich)

Prep Time: 10 mins
Total Time: 20 mins

Servings per Recipe: 2
Calories   872.8
Fat   58.7g
Cholesterol   380.7mg
Sodium   1869.5mg
Carbohydrates   52.4g
Protein   31.7g

Ingredients

4 toaster waffles, toasted
1/2 lb. sausage, made into 2 patties
2 large eggs, beaten

softened butter

Directions

1. Heat a frying pan and cook the sausage patties until cooked through.
2. In another lightly, greased frying pan, cook the eggs until scrambled.
3. Spread the butter on one side of each waffle.
4. Arrange 2 waffles onto serving plate, butter side up and top each with the scrambled egg and sausage patty evenly.
5. Cover with the remaining waffles, buttered side down.

SWEET Mediterranean Waffles

Prep Time: 10 mins
Total Time: 30 mins

Servings per Recipe: 8
Calories   140.4
Fat   3.7g
Cholesterol   69.7mg
Sodium   308.8mg
Carbohydrates   21.6g
Protein   4.8g

Ingredients

1 1/2 C. all-purpose flour
1/2 tsp salt
1 tbsp baking powder
1 tbsp sugar
3 eggs
1 1/2 C. non-fat vanilla yogurt

2 tbsp cinnamon
1 tsp vanilla
1 tbsp oil

Directions

1. Set your waffle iron and lightly, grease it.
2. In a bowl, add the flour and baking powder and mix well.
3. In another bowl, add the yogurt, sugar, eggs, vanilla and salt and beat until well combined.
4. Add the flour mixture and mix until just combined.
5. Add desired amount of the mixture in waffle iron and cook as suggested by the manufacturer.
6. Repeat with the remaining mixture.
7. Enjoy warm.

Cornmeal Cereal Waffles

Prep Time: 10 mins
Total Time: 20 mins

Servings per Recipe: 1
Calories	355.7
Fat	7.0g
Cholesterol	60.9mg
Sodium	307.8mg
Carbohydrates	67.0g
Protein	7.2g

Ingredients

Waffle
- 3 C. Fruit Loops cereal
- 1 3/4 C. all-purpose flour
- 2 tbsp cornmeal
- 1 tbsp sugar
- 1 tbsp baking powder
- 1/4 tsp salt
- 2 eggs
- 2 C. whole milk
- 2 tbsp unsalted butter, cooled

Glaze
- 4 tbsp whole milk
- 2 C. powdered sugar

Directions

1. Set your waffle iron and lightly, grease it.
2. In a blender, add the cereal and pulse until a coarse crumb like mixture is formed.
3. In a bowl, add the cornmeal, flour, sugar, baking powder and salt and mix well.
4. In another bowl, add the milk, butter and eggs and until well combined.
5. Add the flour mixture and stir until just blended.
6. Gently, fold in the cereal crumbs.
7. Add desired amount of the mixture in waffle iron and cook as suggested by the manufacturer.
8. Repeat with the remaining mixture.
9. Meanwhile, for the glaze: in a bowl, add the powdered sugar and milk and beat until smooth.
10. Divide the waffles onto serving plates and top with the glaze.
11. Enjoy warm with a garnishing of the extra cereal.

HONEY
Hazel Waffles

Prep Time: 30 mins
Total Time: 1 hr

Servings per Recipe: 5
Calories	833.7
Fat	45.2g
Cholesterol	203.2mg
Sodium	613.9mg
Carbohydrates	89.9g
Protein	19.5g

Ingredients

1/2 C. unsalted butter
1/4 C. honey
3 1/2 C. all-purpose flour
1 tbsp baking powder
1/2 tsp salt
1/4 tsp baking soda
3 large eggs
1 1/2 C. whole milk

1 C. sour cream
2/3 C. chopped toasted hazelnuts
Pam cooking spray
confectioners' sugar
maple syrup

Directions

1. Set your waffle iron and lightly, grease it.
2. In a pan, add the honey and butter over low heat and cook until melted, stirring frequently.
3. Remove from the heat and keep aside.
4. In a bowl, add the flour, baking soda, baking powder and salt and mix well.
5. In another bowl, add the sour cream, milk and eggs and beat until well combined.
6. Slowly, add the flour mixture and mix until well combined.
7. Add the honey mixture and hazelnuts and gently stir to combine.
8. Add 1 C. of the mixture in waffle iron and cook as suggested by the manufacturer.
9. Repeat with the remaining mixture.
10. Enjoy warm.

Vegetarian Soy Waffles

Prep Time: 5 mins
Total Time: 15 mins

Servings per Recipe: 4
Calories	234.0
Fat	13.3g
Cholesterol	0.0mg
Sodium	491.8mg
Carbohydrates	23.9g
Protein	4.8g

Ingredients

3/4 C. flour
2 tsp baking powder
1/4 tsp salt
1 tsp sugar
1 tbsp ground flax seeds
1/4 C. melted margarine
1 C. soymilk

Directions

1. In a bowl, add the flour, sugar, baking powder and salt and mix well.
2. In another bowl, add the milk, margarine and flax seeds and mix well.
3. Gently, fold the flax seeds mixture into the flour mixture.
4. Add 1/3 C. of the mixture in waffle iron and cook as suggested by the manufacturer.
5. Repeat with the remaining mixture.
6. Enjoy warm.

RACHELA'S
Red Velvet Waffles

Prep Time: 30 mins
Total Time: 40 mins

Servings per Recipe: 4
Calories 662.9
Fat 15.8g
Cholesterol 128.4mg
Sodium 727.7mg
Carbohydrates 117.4g
Protein 14.1g

Ingredients

2 C. flour
1 1/4 C. sugar
1/4 tsp salt
1 tsp baking soda
4 tsp unsweetened cocoa powder
1/4 C. butter, melted, cooled
2 C. buttermilk
2 large eggs, separated

1 tsp vanilla
2 tbsp red food coloring

Directions

1. Set your waffle iron and lightly, grease it.
2. In a bowl, add the flour, sugar, cocoa powder, baking soda and salt and mix well.
3. Add the butter, buttermilk, egg yolks, vanilla and food coloring and mix until well combined.
4. In a glass bowl, add the egg whites and beat until stiff peaks form.
5. Gently, fold the whipped egg whites into the flour mixture.
6. Add desired amount of the mixture in waffle iron and cook as suggested by the manufacturer.
7. Repeat with the remaining mixture.
8. Enjoy warm.

Canadian Chocolate Waffles

Prep Time: 15 mins
Total Time: 25 mins

Servings per Recipe: 1
Calories 357.9
Fat 22.0g
Cholesterol 31.4mg
Sodium 385.1mg
Carbohydrates 38.6g
Protein 7.4g

Ingredients

100 g desiccated coconut
1/2 tsp salt
2 tsp maple syrup
1 tbsp coconut oil
190 g flour, gluten free
25 g unsweetened cocoa powder
1 egg
15 ml maple syrup
1/2 tsp baking soda
5 g baking powder
250 ml milk
60 ml olive oil
1/2 tsp vanilla extract
80 g bittersweet chocolate chips
1 nonstick cooking spray

Directions

1. Set your waffle iron and lightly, grease it.
2. for the coconut butter: in a blender, add the coconut, 2 tsp of the maple syrup, coconut oil and salt and pulse until well combined.
3. In a bowl, add the flour, cocoa powder, baking soda, baking powder and remaining maple syrup and mix until well combined.
4. With a spoon, create a well in the middle of the flour mixture.
5. In the well of the flour mixture, add the oil, milk, egg yolk and vanilla and mix until just blended
6. In a glass bowl, add the egg whites and beat until soft peaks form.
7. Gently, fold the whipped egg whites into the flour mixture.
8. Gently, fold in the chocolate chips.
9. Add desired amount of the mixture in waffle iron and cook for about 3 minutes.
10. Repeat with the remaining mixture.
11. Enjoy warm with a topping of the coconut butter.

CUTE
Waffles

Prep Time: 30 mins
Total Time: 35 mins

Servings per Recipe: 8
Calories	430.2
Fat	19.6g
Cholesterol	181.9mg
Sodium	849.9mg
Carbohydrates	50.5g
Protein	12.3g

Ingredients

6 eggs, separated
1 C. milk
4 C. all-purpose flour
8 tsp baking powder
1 tsp salt

10 tbsp butter, melted
gel food coloring

Directions

1. In a bowl, add the flour, baking powder and salt and mix well.
2. In another bowl, add the milk and egg yolks and beat well.
3. Add the flour mixture and mix until just combined.
4. In a glass bowl, add the egg whites and beat until stiff peaks form.
5. Gently, fold the whipped egg whites into the flour mixture.
6. Now, sift the flour mixture into another bowl.
7. In 6 bowl, divide the mixture evenly.
8. Add enough amount of each color in 1 bowl and stir to combine.
9. In each of 6 Ziploc bag, place 1 colored mixture.
10. Pipe each mixture in circles in waffle iron and cook as suggested by the manufacturer.
11. Enjoy warm.

Vegan Papaya and Orange Waffles

Prep Time: 5 mins
Total Time: 15 mins

Servings per Recipe: 2
Calories   511.7
Fat   23.7g
Cholesterol   0.0mg
Sodium   530.6mg
Carbohydrates   75.8g
Protein   7.4g

Ingredients

- 30 g flour
- 15 g arrowroot
- 15 g coconut flour
- 20 g tiger nuts, or almonds
- 100 g bananas
- 120 g coconut milk
- 20 g water
- 50 g orange juice
- 25 g maple syrup
- 3 g baking soda
- 20 g apple cider vinegar
- 1/2 papaya
- 2 dried figs
- 2 tbsp coconut flakes, shredded
- 10 g dark chocolate, shaved

Directions

1. Set your waffle iron and lightly, grease it.
2. In a bowl, add the flours, arrowroot and tiger nuts and mix until well combined.
3. In a food processor, add the orange juice, coconut milk, water and banana and pulse until well combined.
4. Place the banana mixture and maple syrup in the bowl of the flour mixture and mix until blended nicely.
5. Add in the vinegar and baking soda and mix until blended nicely.
6. Add half of the mixture in waffle iron and cook as suggested by the manufacturer.
7. Repeat with the remaining mixture.
8. Enjoy warm with a topping of the papaya, figs, coconut and chocolate shaving.

SPICY
Cheddar Waffles

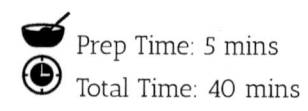

Prep Time: 5 mins
Total Time: 40 mins

Servings per Recipe: 4
Calories   653.6
Fat   36.8g
Cholesterol   155.3mg
Sodium   1041.1mg
Carbohydrates   56.0g
Protein   25.4g

Ingredients

1 C. all-purpose flour
1 C. cornmeal
1 tbsp sugar
1 tbsp baking powder
1 jalapeño, seeded and diced
1/2 tsp kosher salt
2 C. grated sharp cheddar cheese
2 large eggs

1 1/4 C. buttermilk
1/4 C. vegetable oil
nonstick cooking spray

Directions

1. Set your waffle iron and lightly, grease it.
2. In a bowl, add the cornmeal, flour, sugar, baking powder, salt, 1 C. of the cheese and jalapeño and mix well.
3. In another bowl, add the oil, buttermilk and eggs and beat until well combined.
4. Add the flour mixture and mix until just blended.
5. Add 1 1/2 C. of the mixture in waffle iron and cook as suggested by the manufacturer.
6. Repeat with the remaining mixture.
7. Meanwhile, set the broiler of your oven to low and arrange a rack onto a baking sheet.
8. arrange the waffles onto the prepared baking sheet and sprinkle with the remaining 1 C. of the cheese evenly.
9. Cook under the broiler for about 1 minute.
10. Enjoy warm.

Seattle Waffles with Avocados

Prep Time: 15 mins
Total Time: 35 mins

Servings per Recipe: 4
Calories   724.6
Fat   40.0g
Cholesterol   389.4mg
Sodium   1240.5mg
Carbohydrates   67.9g
Protein   25.5g

Ingredients

Waffles
2 C. all-purpose flour
4 tsp baking powder
1 tbsp granulated sugar
1/2 tsp salt
2 large eggs
1 1/2 C. whole milk
1 C. mashed cooked purple sweet potato
3 tbsp vegetable oil
Garnish
2 medium avocados, peeled, pitted and chopped

1 tbsp lime juices
1/2 tsp salt
1/2 tsp black pepper
1/2 tsp crushed red pepper flakes
6 fried eggs
1/2 a red onion, sliced
1/4 C. crumbled feta cheese
2 tbsp chopped parsley

Directions

1. Set your waffle iron and lightly, grease it.
2. For the waffles, in a large bowl, add the flour, sugar, baking powder and salt and mix well.
3. In another bowl, add the remaining ingredients and beat until blended nicely.
4. Add the flour mixture and mix until just combined.
5. Add 1/3 C. of the mixture in waffle iron and cook as suggested by the manufacturer. Repeat with the remaining mixture.
6. Meanwhile, for the topping: in a bowl, add the avocado, lime juice, a pinch of red pepper flakes, salt and pepper and with a fork, mash well.
7. Divide the waffles onto serving plates and top each with a little mashed avocado, followed by 1 fried egg, onion, feta cheese and parsley.
8. Enjoy with a sprinkling of the red pepper flakes.

FULL GEORGIA
Breakfast (Sausage, Waffles, and Home Fries)

Prep Time: 10 mins
Total Time: 35 mins

Servings per Recipe: 4
Calories 843.3
Fat 44.9g
Cholesterol 251.8mg
Sodium 2038.1mg
Carbohydrates 80.3g
Protein 31.0g

Ingredients

Waffles
1/2 C. unsalted butter, melted and cooled
3 large eggs
1 1/2 C. buttermilk
1 tsp vanilla
1 3/4 C. all-purpose flour
2 tsp baking powder
1 tsp baking soda
1/2 tsp salt
1 medium zucchini, shredded
1 (10 oz.) boxes frozen spinach, thawed and well drained
Potatoes
1 (8 oz.) packages beef breakfast sausage
1 C. yellow onion, diced
3 medium Yukon gold potatoes, diced
2 medium carrots, diced
1 small medium bell pepper, diced
1 tsp salt
1/2 tsp black pepper
1/4 C. chopped parsley

Directions

1. For the waffles: in a bowl, add the flour, baking soda, baking powder and salt.
2. In another bowl, add the milk, eggs, butter and vanilla and beat until blended nicely.
3. Add the flour mixture and mix until just moistened.
4. Add the spinach and zucchini and gently, stir to combine.
5. Add 1/3 C. of the mixture in waffle iron and cook as suggested by the manufacturer.
6. Repeat with the remaining mixture.
7. Meanwhile, for the hash, place a wok over medium-high heat until heated through.
8. Add the sausage and cook for about 7 minutes, breaking with a wooden spoon.
9. Add the carrots, potatoes, bell pepper, onion, salt and pepper and stir to combine.
10. Set the heat to medium and cook for about 13-16 minutes, mixing occasionally.
11. Divide the waffles onto serving plates and top each with the sausage hash evenly.
12. Enjoy with a garnishing of the parsley.

Waffles Brulee

Prep Time: 25 mins
Total Time: 55 mins

Servings per Recipe: 1
Calories	733.4
Fat	44.7g
Cholesterol	220.2mg
Sodium	1190.4mg
Carbohydrates	68.1g
Protein	14.8g

Ingredients

Filling
1 lb. cream cheese
1 C. powdered sugar
2 tsp vanilla extract
1 large pinch kosher salt
Waffles
2 C. all-purpose flour
1 tbsp baking soda
1/2 tsp kosher salt

1/4 C. light brown sugar
3 large eggs
2 C. buttermilk
1/2 C. melted unsalted butter
1 tsp vanilla extract
2 1/2 C. turbinado sugar

Directions

1. For the cream cheese filling: in a bowl, add all the ingredients and with a hand mixer, mix until well combined.
2. Set your waffle iron to the medium heat setting and lightly, grease it. For the waffles: in a bowl, add the flour, salt and baking soda and mix well.
3. Add the flour mixture and mix until just combined.
4. In a glass bowl, add the egg whites and beat until medium stiff peaks form. Gently, fold the whipped egg whites into the flour mixture.
5. In the bottom of the heated waffle iron, place about 4 tbsp of the turbinado sugar.
6. Place 1 C. of the waffle mixture over the sugar evenly and top with about 4 tbsp of the filling, followed by 1 tbsp the turbinado sugar.
7. Cook for about 2-3 minutes.
8. With the cooking spray, grease the top of the waffle iron.
9. Place 1 tbsp the turbinado sugar over waffle evenly and cook for about 1 minute further. Repeat with the remaining mixture.
10. Enjoy warm.

SARATOGA
Flax Waffles

🥣 Prep Time: 20 mins
🕐 Total Time: 23 mins

Servings per Recipe: 6
Calories   237.1
Fat   14.1g
Cholesterol   66.0mg
Sodium   612.2mg
Carbohydrates   20.1g
Protein   6.3g

Ingredients

1 C. teff flour
1 C. all-purpose flour
1/4 C. flax seed meal
sugar
1 tbsp baking powder
1 tsp sea salt
1/4 C. vegetable oil
2 eggs
1 tbsp vanilla
1 C. whole milk
fruit

Directions

1. In a bowl, add the flour, flax seed meal, sugar, baking powder and salt and mix well.
2. Add half C. of the milk, oil, eggs and vanilla and mix well.
3. Add the fruit and stir to combine.
4. Add the remaining milk and mix until smooth.
5. Add desired amount of the mixture in waffle iron and cook as suggested by the manufacturer.
6. Repeat with the remaining mixture.
7. Enjoy warm.

Yuan's Chinese Egg Waffles

Prep Time: 5 mins
Total Time: 10 mins

Servings per Recipe: 1
Calories	358.1
Fat	18.3g
Cholesterol	187.1mg
Sodium	410.6mg
Carbohydrates	38.2g
Protein	8.3g

Ingredients

4 eggs, separated
1/4 C. milk
1 tbsp vanilla extract
6 tbsp butter, melted
1/4 C. sugar
1 1/4 C. cake flour
1 1/2 tsp baking powder
1 pinch nutmeg, grated
1/4 tsp salt

canola oil
Garnish
powdered sugar
syrup
fruit
coconut

Directions

1. Set your waffle iron and lightly, grease it.
2. In a bowl, add the flour, nutmeg, baking powder and salt and mix well.
3. In another bowl, add the sugar, milk, butter, egg yolks and vanilla and beat until blended nicely.
4. Add the flour mixture and mix until just combined.
5. In a glass bowl, add the egg whites and beat until stiff peaks form.
6. In 3 additions, gently fold the whipped egg whites into the flour mixture.
7. Add desired amount of the mixture in waffle iron and cook for about 2 minutes per side.
8. Repeat with the remaining mixture.
9. Enjoy warm.

ENJOY THE RECIPES?

KEEP ON COOKING WITH 6 MORE FREE COOKBOOKS!

Visit our website and simply enter your email address to join the club and receive your 6 cookbooks.

http://booksumo.com/magnet

https://www.instagram.com/booksumopress/

https://www.facebook.com/booksumo/

Printed in Great Britain
by Amazon